What Happened at Fatima

by
Leo Madigan

For Lauri and Veronica Duffy, who have
introduced so many to Our Lady of Fatima

All booklets are published thanks to the generous support of the members of the Catholic Truth Society

Blessed Francisco and Jacinta Marto, beatified by Pope John Paul II, 13 May 2000

... I am by birth a shepherd's daughter,

My wit untrained in any kind of art.

Heaven and Our Lady gracious hath it pleased

To shine on my contemptible estate.

Lo! While I waited on my tender lambs,

And to sun's parching head displayed my cheeks,

God's mother deigned to appear to me

And, in a vision full of majesty,

Willed me to leave my base vocation,

And free my country from calamity.

William Shakespeare
(Henry VI Part I. Act I Scene II)

CONTENTS

Introduction

Portugal, in 1917, was a cauldron of political and religious thinking. Godless forces had taken the reins of government, and the Church was represented as a bulwark of superstition. The new thinking, emboldened by the Great War, was all for destroying her influence but it reckoned without the faith of the peasantry, and the concern of heaven, for in this year our blessed Lady stepped in to console, advise, admonish, promise, plead and leave a spiritual perfume that continues to draw millions to the fields where she set her feet.

She came to instigate a revolution and chose the most unlikely candidates imaginable to implement it - three illiterate children from a one-street backwater. These children had little except the values of family, the certainty of faith, and their innocence. It is on these foundations that the Blessed Virgin fashioned them for divine purposes.

Today two of them are among those beatified by Holy Church, indeed, the youngest ever to be honoured. Their joint feastday is observed on 20th February. The third, a cloistered nun in the Carmel of Coimbra, died on 13th February 2005.

But if the choice of peasant children as heaven's messengers is a paradox, that is in keeping with the Message of Fatima itself because heaven's values are opposite to ours. If you can accept that, read on. Indeed, read on even if you find believing difficult.

What Happened at Fatima

The stirring of wings

Some time in 1915 three girls and a boy, aged around 8, were watching their sheep in a rocky olive grove in the hills bordering the western shores of Europe. They ate the lunch they had brought in their shoulder bags then, urged by the natural leader among them, Lucia, they knelt to pray the Rosary.

They had scarcely begun when they saw a figure poised in the air above the trees. It was simply suspended there facing them, though it had no face that the children could see. It looked like a statue made of snow with the rays of the sun playing around it and giving it a patina of transparency.

The children were alarmed, but mesmerised. They continued with their prayer but with their eyes transfixed on the motionless figure above them, which dazzled them with its light.

As they finished their Rosary the figure vanished.

Lucia dos Santos told no one of this strange sighting, but her companions couldn't help but let it all tumble out once they were indoors with their families. In no time, word of the children's strange claim had travelled round Aljustrel, the small, peasant village where they lived. Before long Lucia's mother was questioning her daughter.

"They are saying you saw something up on Cabeço. What was it? What did you see up there?"

Lucia was perturbed as she herself didn't know what she had seen. It wasn't as if the figure had had a face with eyes and a nose and a mouth, or even arms or feet that could be described. Or perhaps it had had these things, but they couldn't be seen because of the light. In her confusion she said, "It looked like a person wrapped up in a sheet."

Her mother, at this point maybe more amused than her show of irritation betrayed, pronounced the claim to be "childish nonsense" and dismissed it.

A week or so later Lucia, with two other children, local boys, was again grazing her flocks on Cabeço and the same white figure, almost transparent in the rays of the sun, appeared hovering above some other trees. The boys saw the vision first and called Lucia's attention to it. As with her previous companions, the boys could not help but tell of it.

And then again, a third time, when Lucia was with her cousin, João Marto, the mysterious form (unseen by João) presided over her prayer, a presence distant yet benign, solemn yet compelling, inexplicable yet accepted without question by the innocent shepherd girl.

Lucia, in her family the youngest of seven children and till this time always the darling, accustomed to the kisses and caresses of her sisters, was suddenly pained to find herself the butt of their jokes. "Are you seeing someone wrapped in a sheet?" they would ask her as she prayed after her First, and subsequent, Communions. "Are these statues of snow skipping around behind your eyes?"

That rural community, Aljustrel in the parish of Fatima, could not possibly have known it, but heaven was schooling one of its children, Lucia dos Santos, preparing her for a role it had selected her to play in one of the most public manifestations of Divine Mercy in our world since Christ walked among us.

The unfolding of the wings

Some time later, in 1916, when Lucia's favourite cousins, Francisco and Jacinta Marto, had permission to shepherd their family flocks, Lucia chose to graze her thirty sheep with theirs on land belonging to branches of their respective families.

One morning when the three children and their sheep were on the hill called Cabeço, a light rain caused them to seek shelter beneath some overhanging rocks. Even when the rain stopped they remained in the comfort of the rocky recess where they ate their lunch and began to say their Rosary. Lucia later recalled that they had got into the habit sometimes of saying only the words Hail Mary! or Our Father! on each bead, so anxious were they to get to the game they called "pebbles". She wasn't sure whether they employed this abbreviated form of the Rosary on this occasion, but soon they were at their game.

Then, without warning, a strong wind began to shake the trees. Since the light rain earlier the sun had been shining and there hadn't even been a breeze. Startled, they looked up and there, above the trees, just as Lucia had seen it before, was the effulgent figure like a statue made of snow.

Neither Francisco nor Jacinta had been with Lucia on the previous occasions when the strange shape had appeared, so they were dumbfounded. The three remained absorbed in this light above the tree tops and, instead of disappearing as it had done before, it began to approach them, floating down from among the branches. As it drew nearer it became clear that it was not a being wrapped in a sheet but a very beautiful youth, about 14 or 15 years old, immaculately white and as transparent as crystal when the sun shines through it.

When his feet touched the ground and he was standing among them he said, "Do not be afraid," just as angels had said to other shepherds near Bethlehem. "I am the Angel of Peace. Pray with me," whereupon he knelt down, bowed until his forehead touched the ground, and said, "My God, I believe, I adore, I hope and I love You! I ask pardon of You for those who do not believe, do not adore, do not hope, and do not love You." He taught the children to repeat the words three times. When he had risen from the ground, and before disappearing, he said to them, "Pray thus. The Hearts of Jesus and Mary are attentive to the voice of your supplication."

This prayer, and the admonition of the angel, penetrated to the very core of their beings so that, thereafter, they spent much of their time in the pasture lands with their sheep prostrate in adoration, repeating its salutation, homage and request over and over again.

Fortunately Lucia, having already suffered on account of the ready tongues of companions, strictly forbade her young cousins to speak to anyone of this encounter and they, despite their tender years, promised silence and maintained it.

It is right to admire their restraint, yet there might be a more subtle reason for their silence than fear of Lucia and that is that their experience, like their intense prayer, though real, was unreal in their daily world. It could have been that on the level of the familiar they were inclined to forget, or at least compartmentalise it. They might have imagined, without specifically thinking it, that conversing with angels was not uncommon, but as nobody spoke about it, neither would they.

Angel at prayer

At the bottom of the garden behind Lucia's home stood a well which the family called Arneiro, which means a dry, barren place. One day during the following summer as Lucia was playing there with Francisco and Jacinta they found, suddenly, that the angel was standing in the midst of them.

"What are you doing?" the angel demanded to know. "Pray, pray very much! The most holy Hearts of Jesus and Mary have designs of mercy on you. Offer prayers and sacrifices constantly to the Most High."

Lucia was understandably puzzled. "How are we to make sacrifices?" she asked.

"Make of everything you can a sacrifice, and offer it to God as an act of reparation for the sins by which he is offended, and in supplication for the conversion of sinners. You will thus draw down peace upon your country. I am its Angel Guardian, the Angel of Portugal. Above all, accept and bear with submission the sufferings which Our Lord will send you."

Whether the Angel of Portugal was the same angel who referred to himself as the Angel of Peace on Cabeço - Lucia thought it was, presumably because they looked the same - we don't know. Some maintain it could have been the Archangel Michael because that celestial figure had long been regarded as National protector by the Portuguese and, given what we know from biblical sources, could also well claim to be an Angel of Peace.[1]

All the time the children kept these things to themselves. They were caught up in a beam of the Divine spotlight that neither they, nor others, not even intimate family, could be expected to appreciate. It is interesting to note that no one seemed to suspect anything out of the ordinary during these months either. Even though the children might have been a little more serious at times, they were equally full of joy and mirth when the time was fitting, as is the way with souls attending to the voice of the Spirit.

So again there was a period of some weeks, perhaps even months, before the angel appeared among them again. This time they had just finished their lunch and had climbed up to their oratory under the overhanging rocks on Cabeço. As soon as they arrived they knelt with their foreheads to the ground, as the angel had shown them, and started praying the Believe, Adore, Hope and Love prayer.

All at once they realised that they were in the midst of a glorious, unearthly light. On raising their heads they saw the angel directly in front of them. In his left hand he held a chalice. Suspended above the chalice was a Sacred Host and from this suspended Host drops of Blood fell into the chalice.

The angel removed his hand from the chalice so that it, too, was suspended in the air and knelt down with them praying. "Most Holy Trinity, Father, Son and Holy Spirit, I adore You profoundly and offer You the most precious Body, Blood, Soul and Divinity of Jesus Christ, present in all the tabernacles of the world, in reparation for the outrages, sacrileges and indifference with which He Himself is offended. And, through the infinite merits of His most Sacred Heart, and the

Immaculate Heart of Mary, I beg of You the conversion of poor sinners."

Three times the children repeated this prayer at the direction of the angel after which the heavenly being rose, took the chalice, presumably in his left hand again, and the Sacred Host in his right. The Host he placed on Lucia's tongue and he shared the Blood from the chalice between Francisco and Jacinta.

As he administered the Sacred Species the angel said, "Eat and drink the Body and Blood of Jesus Christ, horribly outraged by ungrateful men! Make reparation for their crimes and console your God."

The children remained prostrate repeating the Most Holy Trinity prayer until darkness dispersed the light of day over Cabeço at which time they rose and rounded up their sheep to lead them home.

From lunch-time to nightfall! That must have been at least 4-5 hours. 4-5 hours spent in prayer with one's forehead to the ground would suggest a form of ecstasy in a spiritually mature person. In 7 to 10 year olds it couldn't be anything else.

The Lady

And so we come to the late spring, early summer of 1917. 13th May was the day appointed by Providence for the doors of heaven to be unlatched so that the Queen herself might visit earth.

The children took their flocks down the hillside to the north of Aljustrel and across moorland to an area beloning to Lucia's father called Cova da Iria - translated as *peaceful hollow*, or perhaps even as *valley of peace*.

What with the distance - it was a 2 kilometre journey from Aljustrel to Cova da Iria - and the fact that the sheep were grazing on the way, it was getting on for midday before the shepherd children and their flocks arrived at the Cova.

With the sheep settled, the children climbed the slope to the east - where the Basilica now stands - and played at a game of building miniature walls and houses, a pastime for which abundant materials were provided on that rocky terrain.

Suddenly a flash of light arrested them. Although the sky was blue and clear they thought, naturally enough, that it was lightning presaging a summer storm. Their concern was for the sheep and they quickly decided to get the flocks together and lead them home to pen.

Halfway down the slope there was another flash like lightning. A few steps further on and there before them, standing on top of the branches of a young holm-oak tree no more than a metre high, "was a lady all dressed in white. She was more brilliant than the sun and radiated a light clearer and more intense than a crystal glass filled with sparkling water, when the rays of the burning sun shine through it."

The children stopped, nonplussed. They were only a few feet from the lady and bathed in the light which radiated from her.

The lady said, "Do not be afraid, I will do you no harm."

The children did not know that the lady before them was the glorified Mother of Christ herself. They were probably too astounded at this sight which was beyond anything experience or imagination could have prepared them for to have any reaction except stark wonder. Lucia, with hindsight comparing the apparitions of the angel with the Apparitions of Our Lady, spoke of both as transmitting the same intimate joy and peace and happiness; but whereas the angelic presence called for physical prostration, annihilation in the Divine Presence and an awe that rendered her tongue-tied, the presence of Our Lady gave an expansive ease of movement, a joyful exaltation and a communicative enthusiasm.

Lucia said that they were not afraid of the lady but of the thunderstorm they thought was approaching. And yet the lady said, "Do not be afraid, I will do you no harm." There is a strong echo here of the words of the Angel Gabriel to Mary herself at the Incarnation. Now, however, it was her own maternal solicitude that was speaking.

Whatever the children's emotions were, Our Lady's words rallied them, for soon enough Lucia was asking, "Where are you from?" The blunt use of the word "you" doesn't do justice to the Portuguese *vossemecê*, which is an expression of respect from a lower social order to a higher - your worship, your honour, your ladyship.[2]

Lucia's question is delightfully practical. A professional scriptwriter would almost certainly be asking the lady who she was, but for a peasant girl who has just used the word *vossemecê* such a question would be precocious, rude even. But the curiosity of childhood was aroused. Clearly the magnificent being didn't hail from that part of the Ribatejo or even in remote Fatima, or they would have heard of her before. Could there possibly be people as splendid as this in Lisbon, or in other countries?

"I am from heaven."

That must have seemed perfectly reasonable and satisfactory to Lucia. Given the circumstances she may even have suspected it without having had time to register the suspicion. It must also have been clear, too, that this wasn't a social visit. Beings didn't come from heaven to pass the time of day. The lady had something definite to say. And she had chosen to say it to Lucia and her companions. So Lucia asked:

"What do you want of me?" *Vossemecê* again.

"I have come to ask you to come here for six months in succession, on the 13th day, at this same hour. Later on I will tell you who I am and what I want. Afterwards I will return here yet a 7th time." This 7th time is thought to refer to an Apparition which Our Lady is said to have made to Lucia on the eve of her departure for the convent school of Vilar de Porto, 16th June 1921. On that occasion Our Lady had a private message for Lucia.

Lucia, again the practical, enquiring child, asked "Shall I go to heaven too?"

"Yes, you will."

"And Jacinta?"

"She will go also."

"And Francisco?"

"He will go there too, but he must say many Rosaries."

There has been much speculation as to what this means. Some commentators take it to imply that Francisco was a spiritual cut below the two girls and that as a consequence he would have to say half a dozen Rosaries for every one the girls said. But this makes the Rosary out to be a punishment, like lines after school, instead of the sweetest aria in the Marian hymnal. Furthermore, Our Lady's statement that Francisco would have to say many Rosaries surely wasn't tantamount to saying that the girls wouldn't have to say as many as he.

It is important to realise that Francisco couldn't hear what the lady was saying, just as he hadn't been able to hear the angel who had prepared the children for her coming. We have no way of knowing the reason for this and it is fatuous to speculate, but perhaps this codicil of Our Lady's about saying many Rosaries was a special message for him, a message for the girls to pass on later, an earnest reassurance, so to speak, of his equal importance with the girls in the eyes of the Heavenly Visitor. Indeed, when the girls did tell him what Our Lady had said, he crossed his hands on his breast and said, "Oh, my dear Our Lady! I'll say as many Rosaries as you want." (Lucia related this many years later so the "Our Lady" was possibly in hindsight.) Another possibility is that this addition to Our Lady's message for Francisco, far from being a qualification, might have been a diplomatic way of stopping Lucia, entranced like Peter at the Transfiguration, from asking if her mother, father siblings, uncles, neighbours and Kaiser Wilhelm were going to heaven. As it was, her next question was on the same lines, though about a 16 year old who had died a short time before.

"Is Maria das Neves in heaven?"

"Yes, she is."

"And Amélia?"

"She will be in purgatory until the end of the world."

For most of us this is one of the most startling statements of the Apparitions. And it is all the more provoking because it is made without qualification. Amélia was a village girl, about 18 or 20. No one had any reason to doubt that she was any different from others of her age, class and culture. We can assume that she wasn't heading a drug cartel or organising vice rackets. So if an ordinary peasant girl in her late teens must undergo a purgation lasting till the end of the world, when will any of us get to heaven?

Some commentators tell us that "until the end of the world" might, like the biblical 40 days, mean 'a long time.' Others maintain that "till the end of the world" is conditional, that prayers and Masses and the intercession of the Church Militant would temper much of the purgation. This is more easily understood if purgatory is not seen so much as punishment for sin, as a necessary burning away of the foul accretions that sin visits on the soul, a purification of the soul before it can be admitted into the inner household of God. Sin has no substance, it can only be recognised by the pain it causes. We see that in this life and we will see it more clearly in purgatory. The remedy is love. We can only know that by Faith in this life; in purgatory we will understand it and although our love will be absolute according to our capacity, and confirmed, our love will not be able to purify our souls of the accretions because that would be loving ourselves. But the Church Militant, and the Church Triumphant will have powers of intercession here.

There is probably truth in both these explanations but we could do well also to remember that Our Lady is living in eternity and was speaking of something proper to eternity in terms of time. Neither the children nor you nor I could be expected to fully appreciate such measurements.

Our Lady had come to give us a message, and the import of that message is the avoidance of sin and, by implication, of the fires of purgatory, by conforming one's will here in time to the Will of God who dwells in the eternal Now.

One last consideration on this point: Our Lady's mention of purgatory is a stark rebuff to our world, many of whose religious leaders choose to teach that purgatory doesn't exist.

Next - and it could be considered as a comment on the fate of Amélia - Our Lady asked, "Are you willing to offer yourselves to God and bear all the sufferings He wills to send you, as an act of reparation for the sins by which he is offended, and of supplication for the conversion of sinners?"

Observe how Our Heavenly Mother doesn't demand but asks, just as she was asked if she would bear the Messiah. The children could have refused; after all, she had already given her word that they were going to heaven.

"Yes, we are willing!" *Sim, queremos! Fiat!*

"Then you are going to have much to suffer but the grace of God will be your comfort."

At this point Lucia describes a gesture of the Blessed Virgin which was to be repeated at three of the subsequent Apparitions, the significance of which can only be understood in the classroom of prayer. Our Lady opened her hands and communicated a light from them. It was in, and through, that light that the Mediatrix of graces communicated all that she wanted to tell the children. The human words were, in a manner of speaking, simply passing the time of day, a quote for the press. It is when we apply ourselves seriously to study what Lucia tells us about this light and how it affected her and her cousins that we begin to grasp the message of Fatima. It might also explain why Francisco wasn't perturbed about not hearing Our Lady's words - that is because he was fully included in the intense intimacy of these supernatural communications.

Let us listen carefully to what Lucia has to say on the first of these experiences: "As she pronounced these last words ... 'the Grace of God will be your comfort' ... Our Lady opened her hands for the first time, communicating to us a light so intense that, as it streamed from her hands, its rays penetrated our hearts and the innermost depths of our souls, making us see ourselves in God, Who was that light, more clearly than we see ourselves in the best of mirrors. Then, moved by an interior impulse that was also communicated to us, we fell on our knees, repeating in our hearts...'O most Holy Trinity, I adore You! My God, my God, I love you in the most Blessed Sacrament!'"

Notice how the children repeated their prayers in their hearts - not in spoken words.

They had been lifted into a realm that few of us reach in this life, even after long years of faithful prayer; a realm where love is the climate and beauty the landscape, a land where adoration is the currency, the food, the reason for living and the delight of that life. The light showed them God. It showed them themselves in God. The light was God.

There are paradoxes here to cherish and wonder at, concepts to baffle and intrigue which at the same time give vibrant meaning to such phrases as "finding oneself in God" and "a life hidden with Christ in God". Here are images without image, formed of the pure crystal of the spirit, free from the manacle of human words.

Alas, even those caught up in the folds of the mantle of the Queen of Heaven herself must return to feel material soil beneath their feet and hear words spoken from throats.

On the occasion of this first Apparition it was Our Lady who gently released the children from the embrace of ecstasy. She said, "Pray the Rosary every day, in order to obtain peace for the world, and the end of the war."

This is like saying, You have just experienced something of a state of perfection, a peephole into heaven. But you do not live on that plane. You live in a very perilous valley beset by strife and evils. But you can do something about those evils, and strive towards the heaven you have glimpsed, and I'll tell you what it is - "Pray the Rosary every day ..."

Then, says Lucia, she began to rise serenely, going up towards the east, until she disappeared in the immensity of space. The light that surrounded her seemed to open up a path before her in the firmament.

From May to June

After the Lady had departed the children were still bathed in the ecstatic glow of heaven; at the same time they were excited and marvelling. Lucia says that while they were rapt in wonder Jacinta kept breaking into enthusiastic exclamations like:

"Oh what a beautiful Lady!"

Lucia said, "I can see what's going to happen, you'll end up saying that to somebody else."

"No I won't, don't worry."

But she was no sooner home than it all came spilling out to the family. It is easy enough to excuse Jacinta because, after all, she was only a little girl and, although she couldn't have told you, she had just been exposed to one of the greatest phenomena of all time.

But it might be wiser to avoid such condescension. In harmony with the adage, 'Man proposes, God disposes', perhaps her telling of the heavenly encounter was the working of the Holy Spirit. Nothing in her subsequent short life suggests that she was in any way flighty. On the contrary, she seems to have been as obdurate for sanctity as a Thérèse or a Bernadette, enduring a slow martyrdom that would send a mature adult panicking for the morphine bottle. She was also a pre-adolescent child.

As Jacinta herself said when reproached by Lucia the next day, “There was something within me that wouldn’t let me keep quiet.” There is a good argument for that “something” being the Holy Spirit Himself.

Alone with their flocks the children prayed their Rosaries and thought up sacrifices to make in the spirit of the Lady’s request - forgoing water during the heat of the day, giving their lunch to other children, and even to their sheep. But for Lucia the most poignant sacrifice came at home because her mother insisted that she was lying and tried to force her to recant. Although the Marto family was not as harsh with Francisco and Jacinta, it is nonetheless clear to us, looking back on the events as recorded by Lucia, that a way of life was retreating for ever, that the satisfactory, tried and familiar were giving way to the public and the frighteningly unknown. Much misunderstanding, mistrust and emotional upheaval was to be undergone in Aljustrel before the village could accept that three of its children had been chosen as the agents of heaven. And the bulk of this misunderstanding, mistrust and emotional upheaval was to be suffered by the children themselves.

Wednesday, 13th June 1917

The 13th of June is the feast of St Anthony, Portugal’s favourite son, and its patron. It is a time of festivity all over the land but if the adults of Aljustrel had thought the children would forget their claim to have promised to forego the celebrations on that date to return to the Cova da Iria, they were disappointed. The children evinced no interest in the activities associated with the saint. They grazed their sheep in the morning, penned them and then set out by different routes for the Cova. There they waited for their appointment beneath the shade of a great holm-oak (the one that is still standing in the present-day Sanctuary) and reciting the Rosary with the 50 or so people from thereabouts who had joined them.

Promptly at midday they saw the flashes of approaching light. Then there was the Lady standing on the oak sapling, just as she had been a month before.

Lucia was the first to speak. She asked the same question she had asked in May. "What do you want of me?" *Vossemecê* again.

"I wish you to come here on the 13th of next month, to pray the Rosary every day, and to learn to read. Later I will tell you what I want."

The first two of these injunctions had already been given in the first Apparition. To learn to read is a surprising but practical charge in as much as Lucia was to be Heaven's instrument to communicate the Fatima message to the world.

Lucia asked for the cure of a sick person.

"If he is converted he will be cured during the year."

Lucia's next question, intriguingly, reveals something of the state of the children's minds. The Lady had beguiled them; the God they saw themselves in when the rays from the Lady's hands penetrated their hearts had beguiled them; heaven itself had beguiled them. The supernatural had kidnapped their every thought and affection. They had been promised heaven, had even been given a glimpse of it and now all else was insipid. They were hungry and there was no point in lingering outside the dining room when the food was already on the table.

"I would like to ask you to take us to heaven."

This is not a spontaneous, "Please take us to heaven," or an "I ask you to take us to heaven". It is a planned question. The words have been carefully thought out, chosen, because everything depends on their reception. The children, one could almost wager, had spent a great deal of time since the last Apparition formulating these words. They had no way of knowing, of course, that in their simplicity they had devised what could arguably be the most perfect of petitionary prayers - "I would like to ask you to take us to heaven."

The Lady answered, "Yes. I will take Jacinta and Francisco soon. But you are to stay here some time longer. Jesus wishes to make use of you to make me known and loved. He wants to establish in the world devotion to my Immaculate Heart. I promise salvation to those who embrace it, and those souls will be loved by God like flowers placed by me to adorn his throne." The true beauty and magnificence of such a statement can only be apprehended here by deep meditation on the words, and only fully appreciated when the promise itself is realised in heaven.

"Am I to stay here alone?" Not only is Lucia deprived of an early entry into the place where her heart is, but she is to be separated from the two companions who have shared the divine experience. There could be no others, not if she searched every house in the world. In that sense she would be as alone as if she had been abandoned in a far galaxy. One is reminded of the trial of Joan of Arc when the belligerent Bishop Cauchon asked, "Did you see the Archangel and the attendant angels in the body, or in the spirit?" and Joan answered, "I saw them with the eyes of my body, just as I see you; and when they went away I cried because they did not take me with them."

But the Lady answered, "No my daughter. Are you suffering a great deal? Don't lose heart. I will never forsake you. My Immaculate Heart will be your refuge and the way that will lead you to God."

Comfort indeed, and endorsed immediately because, as in May, the Lady - I think we can say Our Lady now -opened her hands and communicated to the children the rays of the same intense light. Again they saw themselves immersed in God. "Jacinta and Francisco," Lucia says, "seemed to be in that part of the light which rose towards heaven, and I in that which was poured out on the earth. In front of the palm of Our Lady's right hand was a Heart encircled by thorns which pierced it. We understood that this was the Immaculate Heart of Mary, outraged by the sins of humanity, and seeking reparation."

Because he couldn't hear Our Lady's words Francisco didn't understand the significance of the Heart. He asked later, "Why did Our Lady have a Heart in her hand, spreading out over the world that great light which is God? You were with Our Lady in the light which went down towards the earth, and Jacinta was with me in the light which rose towards heaven!"

"That is because you and Jacinta will soon go to heaven while I, with the Immaculate Heart of Mary, will remain for some time longer on earth." Note how there is no longer talk of Lucia being alone.

"How many years longer will you stay here?"

"I don't know. Quite a lot."

"Was it Our Lady who said so?"

"Yes, and I saw it in the light that she shone into our hearts."

And Jacinta endorsed Lucia, "It is just like that! That's exactly how I saw it too!"

Francisco said, "These people are so happy just because you told them that Our Lady wants the Rosary said, and that you are to learn to read! How would they feel if they only knew what she showed to us in God, in her Immaculate Heart, in that great light! But this is a secret. It must not be spoken about. It is better that no one should know it."

From 13th June to 13th July 1917

The period between the June and the July Apparitions was one of doubt and perplexity for the children - not doubt about the reality of their experiences but, for Lucia, doubt as to their source and, for her cousins, perplexity at the contrary attitude of adults.

Lucia also appears to have borne the brunt of the taunts of siblings and peers. It was perceived that she, the eldest of the three and a natural leader, was spinning a web of intrigue, manipulating Francisco and Jacinta into it as if into a secretive clique. Lucia's mother was particularly opposed to her daughter's claims. She was adamant that Lucia was lying. She scolded, threatened and, at times, gave Lucia the silent treatment which distressed the sensitive ten year old, used to nothing but displays of trust and affection.

Eventually Maria Rosa, Lucia's distracted mother, took her daughter - while her brother Ti Marto took his children Francisco and Jacinta - to be interviewed by the Parish Priest.

The outcome of that encounter was an agony for Lucia. Fr Ferreira reasoned that Our Lady would hardly come from heaven to tell people to say the Rosary every day - a practice which was wide-spread in the area anyway - and furthermore that genuine communications from heavenly sources usually told visionaries to reveal every aspect of the encounter to a confessor as a guard against illusion. These children spoke of secrets and were far from willing to answer every question candidly. Their visions, he said, if indeed they were experiencing visions, may well be of satanic origin.

Lucia was devastated. Horrific doubts swamped her young mind. The suffering she had agreed to embrace had become a gargantuan reality. One paragraph in the memoirs brings this anguish into stark relief: "While in this state of mind, I had a dream which only increased the darkness of my spirit. I saw the devil laughing at having deceived me, as he tried to drag me down to hell. On finding myself in his clutches, I began to scream so loudly and call on Our Lady for help that I awakened my mother. She called out to me in alarm, and asked me what was the matter. I can't recall what I told her, but I do remember that I was so paralysed with fear that I couldn't sleep any more that night. This dream left my soul clouded over with real fear and anguish. My one relief was to go off by myself to some solitary place, there to weep to my heart's content. Even the company of my cousins began to seem burdensome, and for that reason, I began to hide from them as well. The poor children! At times they would search for me, calling out my name and receiving no answer, but I was there all the while, hidden right close to them in some corner where they never thought of looking."

She even considered agreeing with her mother and saying that the whole episode was a lie but Jacinta told her, "No, It's not the devil! Not at all. They say that the devil is very ugly and that he's down under the ground in hell. But that Lady is so beautiful, and we saw her go up to heaven!"

Lucia had decided not to go to the Cova on July 13th and she held to this decision right up to the moment when it was time for them to leave. "I suddenly felt," she writes, "that I had to go, impelled by a strange force that I could hardly resist."

Friday, 13th July 1917

Independent of the disbelief and hostility shown to the children, word of the alleged Apparitions had burst the bounds of the Fatima parish and some three or four thousand people had assembled in the Cova on the 13th of July. When the children arrived these pilgrims were saying the Rosary, many of them on their knees.

There was no waiting. As soon as they reached the sapling they saw light flashes signifying the approach of their heavenly visitor. A moment later and Our Lady was standing on the little tree.

Again Lucia asked, "What do you want of me?"

"I want you to come here on the 13th of next month, to continue to pray the Rosary every day, in honour of Our Lady of the Rosary, in order to obtain peace for the world and the end of the war, because only she can help you."

The puzzling thing about this statement is the use of the third person. Our Lady is speaking and yet she refers to herself as if she was someone else. This may well be because she still hasn't told the shepherds who she is - though if Lucia's memory was accurate and not merely a slip of hindsight, they were already calling her Our Lady among themselves. Or, in a way that is difficult for us to understand, perhaps, in the hierarchy of heaven the various aspects of Mary are seen as individual as they are when we invoke them in the litanies. But if this is so we can be sure that they complement each other wholly. Or maybe the word "I" doesn't exist in heaven except in God's "I am who am" definition of Himself.

"I would like to ask you to tell us who you are, and to work a miracle so that everybody will believe that you are appearing to us."

Here again the sentence sounds rehearsed. This "tell us who you are" could mean, "confirm that you are Our Lady" or "remove any doubts I have that you really are from heaven and not a diabolical illusion."

The "work a miracle", while rehearsed is, paradoxically, a spontaneous act of filial confidence glowing with the boldness of naivety. If you or I, or the House of Representatives asked for a miracle, we shouldn't be surprised if the question was ignored and we were humiliated. With these children the answer is as candid as the question.

"Continue to come here every month. In October I will tell you who I am and what I want, and I will perform a miracle for all to see and believe." True, Our Lady is using "I" here but she is, for the moment, on earth, speaking an earthly language to earthlings.

Many people had asked Lucia to ask Our Lady to cure their, or their families', ailments and she took this opportunity to petition the Apparition. Our Lady replied that these people must pray the Rosary in order to obtain these graces during the year. Then she added, though as a major part of the message rather than as a postscript: "Sacrifice yourself for sinners, and say many times, especially when you make some sacrifice: 'O Jesus, it is for love of You, for the conversion of sinners, and in reparation for sins committed against the Immaculate Heart of Mary.'"

It is not possible, except in the higher realms of infused prayer, to give God our full, moment by moment attention in this life, but we can give our full intention, and with this prayer Our Heavenly Mother seems to be implying this. Alas! the corollary is also true. It can be an intention to deprive God of His paternal rights over us - that is, to sin - and few things could be more deeply hurtful to the heart of a mother than rebellion in the family.

Now, for the third time, Our Lady opened her hands to emit the light of God. This time the aspect of eternity the children were shown was not the rapturous sight of themselves plunged into the Will of God, but hell.

Lucia says, "The rays of light seemed to penetrate the earth, and we saw, as it were, a sea of fire. Plunged in this fire were demons and souls in human form, like transparent burning embers, all blackened or burnished bronze, floating about in the conflagration, now raised into the air by the flames that issued from within themselves together with great clouds of smoke, now falling back on every side like sparks in huge fires, without weight or equilibrium, amid shrieks and groans of pain and despair, which horrified us and made us tremble with fear. The demons could be distinguished by their terrifying and repellent likeness to frightful and unknown animals, black and transparent like burning coals. Terrified and as if to plead for succour, we looked up at Our Lady, who said to us, so kindly and so sadly:

'You have seen hell where the souls of poor sinners go. To save them, God wishes to establish in the world devotion to my Immaculate Heart. If what I say to you is done, many souls will be saved and there will be peace. The war is going to end; but if people do not cease offending God, a worse one will break out during the pontificate of Pius XI. When you see a night illuminated by an unknown light, know that this is the great sign given you by God that he is about to punish the world for its crimes, by means of war, famine and persecutions of the Church and of the Holy Father.

'To prevent this, I shall come to ask for the consecration of Russia to my Immaculate Heart, and the Communion of Reparation on the First Saturdays. If my requests are heeded, Russia will be converted, and there will be peace; if not, she will spread her errors throughout the world, causing wars and persecutions of the Church. The good will be martyred, the Holy Father will have much to suffer, various nations will be annihilated. In the end, my Immaculate Heart will triumph. The Holy Father will consecrate Russia to me, and she will be converted, and a period of peace will be granted to the world. In Portugal, the dogma of the Faith will always be preserved...'"

Then Our Lady showed the children a vision which was for long known as the third secret of Fatima. In the words of Cardinal Sodano: "It is a prophetic vision similar to those found in Sacred Scripture, which do not describe with photographic clarity the details of future events, but rather synthesise and condense against a unified background events spread out over time in a succession and duration which are not specified. The result must be interpreted in a symbolic key."

Here is the official text of the letter written by Lucia on 3rd January 1944 referring to the third part of the "secret," the prophetic vision revealed to the seers on 13th July 1917.

"I write in obedience to you, my God, who command me to do so through His Excellency the Bishop of Leiria and through your Most Holy Mother and Mine.

"After the two parts which I have already explained, at the left of Our Lady and a little above, we saw an angel with a flaming sword in his left hand; flashing, it gave out flames that looked as though they would set the world on fire; but they died out in contact with the splendour that Our Lady radiated towards him from her right hand: pointing to the earth with his right hand, the angel cried out in a loud voice: "Penance, Penance, Penance!" And we saw in an immense light that is God: 'something similar to how people appear in a mirror when they pass in front of it', and a Bishop dressed in white: 'we had the impression that it was the Holy Father'. Other Bishops, Priests, men and women religious going up a steep mountain, at the top of which there was a big cross of rough-hewn trunks as of a cork tree with the bark; before reaching there the Holy Father passed through a big city half in ruins and half trembling with halting step, afflicted with pain and sorrow, he prayed for the souls of the corpses he met on his way; having reached the top of the mountain, on his knees at the foot of the big Cross he was killed by a group of soldiers who fired bullets and arrows at him, and in the same way there died one after another the other Bishops, Priests, men and women religious, and various lay people of different ranks and positions. Beneath the two arms of the Cross there were two Angels each with a crystal aspersorium in his hand, in which they gathered up the blood of the Martyrs and with it sprinkled the souls that were making their way to God.

Cardinal Sodano said that the "Bishop clothed in white who falls to the ground, apparently dead under a burst of gunfire, is a prophesy of the attempt on the life of Pope John Paul II in Rome on 13th May 1981." The Pope himself has spoken of "a motherly hand which guided the bullet's path enabling him to halt at the threshold of death."

It is interesting to note that Karol Wojtyla, who was to become Pope John Paul II, was not born when the prophecy was made.

"Do not tell this to anybody. Francisco, yes, you may tell him.

"When you pray the Rosary, say, after each mystery: 'O my Jesus, forgive us, save us from the fires of hell. Lead all souls to heaven, especially those who are most in need.'"

After a silence Lucia asked, "Is there anything more that you want of me?"

"No, I do not want any more of you today."

Again she rose towards the east and disappeared.

Although Our Lady has said that she will reveal who she is and what she wants in the October Apparition, she immediately speaks of her Immaculate Heart, which could hardly indicate any other woman, and gives some pretty blunt details of what she wants done. It is as if the matter is of such urgency, and her love so strong, that even the Queen of Heaven can't be constrained into keeping her own deadline.

Lucia, Francisco and Jacinta in 1917. By kind permission of D Luciano Coelho Cristino, Fatima Sanctuary.

The strongest impression made on Francisco in this Apparition was not so much the vision of Hell as the perception of God, the Most Holy Trinity, seen in that light from Our Lady's hands which penetrated their souls. Afterwards Lucia records him as saying, "We were on fire with that light which is God, and yet we were not burnt! What is God?... We could never put it into words. Yes, that is something indeed which we could never express! But what a pity it is that He is so sad! If only I could console Him!"

Monday, 13th August 1917

The children didn't see Our Lady on the 13th of that August because they were not at the Cova. It happened like this.

On the morning of the 13th August the Mayor of Ourem, the administrative centre of the area which included Fatima, sent a message to Lucia's house to say that he was waiting to interview her at the house of her cousins. Lucia and her father made their way through the crowds which swamped the short distance between the two houses. All month, since the July Apparition, great numbers of people had been descending on Aljustrel to see the seers, to speak with them, to press a petition for the Virgin. They were almost intolerable. "In the middle of that crowd", says Lucia with her happy knack for an image, "we were like a ball in the hands of boys at play."

The Mayor of Ourem, Artur de Oliveira Santos, wa 26 at the time of the apparitions. The locals called hir the Tinker because he'd made his money in the manner c what we might call a scrap-metal dealer. As a member o the Leiria Masonic Lodge he founded a branch in Ouren and got himself appointed President of the Municipa Chamber and, although lacking any legal training, Judge Substitute in the area.

A contemporary photograph shows this fellow lookin a bit like Humphrey Bogart with a monocle. His stanc has all the confident certitude of the new thinking, of th politically progressive - anti-monarchism, anti-medieva superstition, anti-cant - all of which would add up to anti Church. Secularism, anti-conservatism, every shiny nev "ism" that speaks of a world ordained by the Republi for man, in the name of man, radiated from Artur' brow. He and his wife Idalina had eight children, whic is admirable. He gave them names like Victor Hugo Democracia, Franklin etc, which tells us quite a bit.

Here, in his very own territory, a plague of religiou fervour was breaking out. It was Artur's duty to hi beliefs, his Lodge, his continuance in his exalted post, t quash it decisively, once and for all.

The Mayor had arrived at the Marto home with glib offer to take the children to the Cova in his horse drawn carriage. He said he would like to see the miracl himself so that he could believe, like St Thomas. At tha point the three children came into the room, but they declined his offer. He insisted, saying that with him they could avoid the crowds. When they still declined he insisted further, adding that they would go by way of Fatima Church because he wished to consult with the parish priest, Fr Ferreira.

At the priest's house the Mayor separated the children, taking Lucia inside and leaving Francisco and Jacinta in the carriage. Then, after a short while, he emerged from the priest's house, hastily marshalled Lucia into the carriage and trotted the horse off in the direction of the Cova. At the main road, however, he turned to the right and whipped the horse off to a speed towards Ourem.

Artur de Santos had kidnapped the three seers.

The many thousands who had gathered in the Cova did hear thunder and some saw the flashes of light and 'a little cloud, very delicate, very white, which stopped for a few moments over the tree and then rose in the air and disappeared". However, when word got about that the children had been abducted there was a near riot. In the meantime the children had been taken to the Mayor's house where his wife, a motherly woman, treated them to a fine meal and set them to play with her own offspring.

But the Mayor was determined to get the secret out of them and the next morning, a Tuesday, the interrogation started in his offices. They were offered money and blandishments, but nothing would move them. In the afternoon the Mayor worked on them again with more menace but they remained as uncommunicative as they had been from the outset.

It was at this point, some thirty hours after they had been taken from Fatima, that the cousins were actually thrown into the communal cell which comprised the town's public jail. Their captor told them that they were to remain there while a cauldron of oil was being boiled. Unless they relented and confided their secret to him they were to be executed by being thrown into it.

I wonder if any childhood nightmare could equate with the dread and anguish of Lucia, Francisco and Jacinta during the two hours they spent in this confinement. For us it might seem a nasty experience, though of a piece with this encounter between good and evil, between pride and obedience, between conflicting wills. And two hours isn't all that long, we might say. But the cousins didn't know how long they were to remain in the fetid cell with a mêlée of adult prisoners. It was an atrium of death. Their bodies were to be plunged into boiling oil. (Our minds cannot encompass the horror at will; think of it next time you are dipping your toe into the bathwater to test the temperature.) This is no child's bogeyman nightmare. As far as they were concerned it was a reality and, to compound the agony, for the first time in their lives they were separated from the familiar - mother, father, family, all that young lives hold dear.

Their fellow prisoners tried, naturally enough, to induce them to tell the Mayor their secret, indeed to tell him any old thing to get themselves released. You and I would probably have enjoyed concocting an elaborate fiction to beguile the bureaucratic, self-opinionated man, but the cousins had glimpsed the Truth, and anything less than the Truth was no longer an option.

One of the prisoners had an accordion and soon they were singing songs, and even dancing. Then Jacinta took a medal from her pocket and, placing it on a nail on the wall, knelt with her cousins to say the Rosary. They met with no opposition from the other prisoners; indeed, in no time they, too, were on their knees in prayer.

It is recorded that one of them kept his hat on. Francisco said to him, "When you pray you must take your hat off." The fellow, doubtless feeling awkward enough on his knees and now being instructed by a 9 year old, wrenched the hat from his head and threw it on the floor. Francisco picked it up for him and placed it gently on a bench.

The guards returned with the awful summons. The cell door was unlocked and the children taken to the Mayor. Further interrogation led nowhere. They were locked in another room and presently removed one by one, presumably to the vat of boiling oil. Jacinta was first. Some time after the guard returned to announce that Jacinta was already scalding to death and he took

Francisco. Left alone, Lucia suffered a pre-execution agony which must have been, I hazard, worse than the execution itself.

But when she was taken from the room it was not to her death at all, but into the arms of her cousins.

Artur de Oliveira Santos tried further tricks to draw th secret from them but their resolve had been strengthened by the grace attendant on the ordeal they had withstood.

The main parts of what we are referring to as "the secret - secret in the sense that Our Lady didn't wish them to communicate things she had confided to them until she herself was ready to let them do so - comprised: (1) the knowledge that Francisco and Jacinta would die young but that Lucia would stay on earth longer; (2) their sight of hell and (3) the prophetic vision which included "the Bishop clothed in white". It is interesting to speculate what the Tinker would have made of it had the children been given leave to tell him. I suspect it would have swollen the man' self esteem to be able to boast that he had broken their resolve and also that he would have dismissed the material itself as the Portuguese equivalent of "fiddlesticks" - precisely the same reaction that the world extends to all heavenly advances.

That night the children slept again at the Mayor' house and the next day, a Wednesday, the feast of the Assumption of Our Blessed Lady, he took them back to Fatima in his carriage and deposited them on the veranda of the presbytery.

Sunday, 19th August 1917

On the following Sunday afternoon Lucia was grazing her flock in Valinhos, near Aljustrel. Francisco was with her, and his elder brother João. Around four o'clock Lucia sensed the approach of the supernatural. There was a flash of the heralding light and she sent João to fetch Jacinta who arrived in time for the second flash and the appearance of the Virgin on another holm-oak sapling.

Lucia asked the customary question, "What do you want of me?"

"I want you to continue going to the Cova da Iria on the 13th, and to continue praying the Rosary every day. In the last month, I will perform a miracle so that all may believe."

This is as much as Lucia records in the Memoirs. Given the degree of intimacy that had built up between Our Lady and Lucia, as spokesman for the children, a practise of easy, though reverent, question and request, it seems odd that Lucia makes no mention of their failure to be at the Cova on Monday 13th August, or of some indication from Our Lady that she was aware that their absence had been through no fault of their own. Many writers on the subject report that Our Lady said that because they had been abducted and taken to Ourem, the miracle intended for October would be less great. There doesn't appear to be any evidence for this claim in the Memoirs. Confusion might have arisen when João reported to Dr. Formigão the following November, that Lucia had told him that Our Lady had said that the miracle would be better known because of the abduction.

"What do you want done with the money the people leave in the Cova da Iria?"

"Have two litters made. One is to be carried by you and Jacinta and two other girls dressed in white; the other one is to be carried by Francisco and three other boys. The money from the litters is for the "festa" of Our Lady of the Rosary, and what is left over will help towards the construction of a chapel that is to be built here."

"I would like to ask you to cure some sick persons."

"Yes, I will cure some of them during the year."

Then, as Lucia comments, looking very sad, Our Lady said, "Pray, pray very much, and make sacrifices for sinners; for many souls go to hell, because there are none to sacrifice themselves and to pray for them."

This is an explosive statement and one that can only be appreciated after allowing it to marinate in the wine of personal prayer. (It is a matter of continual astonishment, even for wholly dedicated and enlightened souls, that it is part of the divine dispensation that God relies on man to ask for grace.) For the children it must have been that much more alarming because the vision of hell which they been shown in July was still vivid in their minds.

There was no light from Our Lady's hands at this unscheduled Apparition; she simply rose and disappeared towards the east. João, who was present, said that he saw and heard nothing except "a noise that sounded like a rocket" at this departure.

From August to September 1917

The days between the Apparitions seemed to swirl with people wanting to see and speak with the seers, and the seers themselves trying desperately to be alone and to make sacrifices to console the "Hidden Jesus" and the Immaculate Heart of Mary offended by the indifference of man. Home life had been disturbed almost beyond repair.

Lucia records that some days after the August Apparition at Valinhos... "as we were walking along the road with our sheep, I found a piece of rope that had fallen off a cart. I picked it up and, just for fun, I tied it round my arm. Before long I noticed that this rope was hurting me. 'Look, this hurts!' I said to my cousins. 'We could tie it round our waists and offer this sacrifice to God.'

"The poor children promptly fell in with my suggestion. We then set about dividing it between the three of us, by placing it across a stone and striking it with the sharp edge of another one that served as a knife. Either because of the thickness or roughness of the rope, or because we sometimes tied it too tightly, this instrument of penance often caused us terrible suffering. Now and then, Jacinta could not keep back her tears, so great was the discomfort this caused her. Whenever I urged her to remove it, she replied, "No! I want to offer this sacrifice to Our Lord in reparation, and for the conversion of sinners."

This was but one of dozens of sacrifices they devised as they stumbled in their childlike way to placate their Heavenly Mother and the Hidden Jesus.

Thursday, 13th September 1917

A crowd estimated at around thirty thousand had assembled in the Cova when the children walked there for their September assignation. It was almost a miracle in itself that they got to the holm-oak for midday as the crowds pressed in on them all the way, clutching at them, kneeling on the ground before them, begging for intercession to be made for themselves or their loved ones. People who could not get near shouted through the crowd, asking for a cure for a blind son, a deaf daughter, a crippled spouse. Like Zacchaeus in the sycamore tree as Christ entered Jericho, they climbed walls and branches to catch a glimpse of the children and call out their petitions.

It is interesting to note that the behaviour of the vast crowds gathered there, without any organising body at all, was said to have been a profound demonstration of faith, a pilgrimage worthy of the name. At the site almost everyone was kneeling and saying the Rosary with devotion, the men with uncovered heads.

The edifying deportment of the crowds notwithstanding, someone in the press with scissors snipped off Lucia's plaits which she wore down to her waist. She says that her mother was most upset when she saw that she had even less hair than Francisco. But, she comments, "nothing is my own, so what of it! Everything belongs to God. May he dispose all as best pleases Him."

When the children finally arrived they had not long started on the Rosary themselves before a flash of light from the east announced the approach of Our Lady, and shortly she was there among them, standing on the tree.

Our Lady said, "Continue to pray the Rosary in order to obtain the end of the war. In October Our Lord will come, as well as Our Lady of Dolours and Our Lady of Carmel. St Joseph will appear with the Child Jesus to bless the world. God is pleased with your sacrifices. He does not want you to sleep with the rope on, but only to wear it during the day time."

"I was told to ask you many things, the cure of some sick people, of a deaf-mute..."

"Yes, I will cure some, but not others. In October I will perform a miracle so that all may believe."

Although Lucia doesn't mention it in the Memoirs, she told the parish priest two days after the event that Our Lady had said here, "I will cure some, but not others because Our Lord does not trust them." Also during the same apparition, Lucia told the parish priest that she offered the Blessed Virgin some letters with a bottle of scented water saying, "They gave me this if you *(vossemecê)* would like them." The gifts were declined, very graciously considering, with the words, "This is not needed in heaven" *(Isso não é conveniente lá para o ceu)*.

As in the previous month there were no rays from the Virgin's hands. She simply rose and went off to the east.

There were many reports at the time of two further phenomena at this apparition, though Lucia does not mention them in her Memoirs. The first occurred before the appearance of Our Lady. Apparently the sky darkened around noon. A witness declared, "It was as if dusk had fallen very quickly and I thought I could make out the stars, as if it were really nightfall. Some of the crowd cried, "Look!" and the people saw what was known at the time as the prodigy of the ball of fire." The future vicar-general of Leiria, Padre João Quaresma, gave the following testimony: "To my great astonishment I saw, clearly and distinctly, a luminous globe coming from the east and moving to the west, gliding slowly and majestically through space. With my hand I motioned to Monsignor Gois who was standing next to me, and who had been making fun of me for coming. Looking up he too saw this unexpected vision. Then suddenly this globe, giving off an extraordinary light, disappeared from my sight, and Monsignor Gois, also, saw it no longer. But there was a little girl, dressed like Lucia and of about the same age, who continued to cry happily, 'I see it! I see it! Now it is coming down towards the bottom of the hill.' It was a luminous globe, according to those who saw it, oval in form and with the widest part underneath."

It is interesting to note that Canon Manuel Nunés Formigão, the interrogator of the seers and the first champion of Fatima, was present and saw nothing at all of this globe.

The second phenomenon, which seems to have occurred as Our Lady departed towards the east, was even more striking. It was a fall of white petals which, "like round, shining snowflakes floated down towards the earth, in a strong beam of preternatural light." Contrary to the laws of perspective these petals became smaller as they fell. They vanished as they reached the people, leaving no trace.

This took place not only on this day of the September apparition, but also during pilgrimages to Fatima on 13th May 1918 and again on 13th May 1924.

Saturday, 13th October 1917

It doesn't require much imagination to picture the pressure put on the children, their families and their village, before the October Apparition. When the 13th arrived an estimated 70,000 people turned up in appalling weather conditions in this remote hill country that was barely equipped to sustain its few villages and livestock. 70,000 would be a dream number for a sponsored event nowadays but in 1917, long before television and radio, to say nothing of mass transport, a crowd of 70,000 must have been an awesome sign of man's hankering for the supernatural.

The difficulty the children had getting through the crowds to the tree has been well documented, each report mentioning the word 'torrential' when describing the rain that poured from the sky, making a mud bath of the entire Cova.

Once at the arch erected by the local people on the Apparition sight - the tree had been denuded by souvenir seekers - Lucia, moved as she says by an interior impulse, asked the people to shut their umbrellas and say the Rosary.

It might be appropriate here to mention another phenomenon, visible to all the people, and well documented at the time, a thin, well-defined column of blue smoke, rising to a height of about six metres. It appeared on the occasion of each apparition and on this last was said to be visible from as far off as the district highway with perfect clarity. It was visible to the naked eye and lasted for approximately a minute. The smoke would dissipate but after a little while would return a second and a third time. One of the many witnesses to the parish enquiry, Jacinto de Almeida Lopes, later attested that he "saw, above the people, twisting around the oak several times, and rising up by itself, a single little cloud of smoke - like smoke from a thurible at the time of incensing, or the smoke of a cigarette. At first I thought that there was someone there who was smoking, or making a fire to keep warm, but then I realised that there was no such fire over there."

However, soon the children were aware of the flash of the Virgin's approach and then they saw her in her customary position.

"What do you want of me?"

"I want to tell you that a chapel is to be built here in my honour. I am the Lady of the Rosary. Continue always to pray the Rosary every day. The war is going to end, and the soldiers will soon return to their homes."

"I have many things to ask you: the cure of some sick persons, the conversion of sinners, and other things..."

"Some yes, but not others. They must amend their lives and ask forgiveness for their sins."

Then, Lucia writes: "looking very sad, Our Lady said, 'Do not offend the Lord our God any more, because He is already so much offended.'"

Elsewhere in the Memoirs she comments on this sentence: "How loving a complaint, how tender a request! Who will grant me to make it echo through the whole world, so that all the children of our Mother in heaven may hear the sound of her voice?"

Our Lady then began to ascend towards the east but while doing so she opened her hands as she had done in the first three Apparitions and made them reflect on the sun. As she moved back to heaven the reflection of her own light continued to be projected onto the sun itself.

At this point Lucia cried out, "Look at the sun!" She says that she was moved by an interior impulse to say this and that she herself was not aware of the sun or even of the presence of the people. She gives no account of the famous "Miracle of the Sun" because she didn't see it. Neither did Francisco nor Jacinta. (João - who actually died, aged 94, as this paragraph was being written, Friday, 28.4.00, a fortnight before the beatification of his younger siblings - was at home hiding under the bed in fear of the lynching that he imagined was to come when there was no miracle to satisfy the people.) Lucia tells what they saw while the assembled 70,000 watched the solar fireworks.

"After Our Lady had disappeared into the immense distance of the firmament," she writes, "we beheld St Joseph with the Child Jesus and Our Lady robed in white with a blue mantle, beside the sun. St Joseph and the Child Jesus appeared to bless the world, for they traced the Sign of the Cross with their hands. When, a little later, this Apparition disappeared, I saw Our Lord and Our Lady; it seemed to me that it was Our Lady of Dolours. Our Lord appeared to bless the world in the same manner as St Joseph had done. This Apparition also vanished, and I saw Our Lady once more, this time resembling Our Lady of Carmel.

What the people saw in the Cova da Iria that October midday is very well documented and can be found in any number of books. It is interesting to note, however, that no two accounts concur exactly. With such a phenomenon this is not surprising; astonishment, fear, exaltation and plain old imagination must have all played conspicuous roles in both the observing and in the retelling.

However the student of these reports cannot help but entertain the suspicion that every individual saw something different. The template was the same but each experience of it was unique. It is the same with prayer. No two people have the same approach to God in prayer, or the same experience as a response. And there will be as many explanations for the phenomenon as there are people. It is more profitable, perhaps, to ponder these things in our hearts.

Some suggest that St Joseph's appearance in this great October vision of Fatima might indicate that his body, too, was taken to heaven after his death. It is an attractive thought to the devout, but one which disorientates theologians. The Church has never said a word on the subject, and until she does we can assume that St Joseph himself would prefer we dwell on the truths she teaches and not to busy ourselves with speculation.

The miracle of the Sun

Of the 70,000 eyewitnesses at the Cova da Iria that October midday, and the many others in towns and villages around who witnessed what has become known as the Miracle of the Sun, many wrote down their impressions. Here are a few extracts from those records.

The children had foretold the day and the hour at which the solar phenomenon would occur. The news spread rapidly throughout Portugal and in spite of bad weather thousands and thousands of people congregated at the spot. At the hour of the last Apparition they witnessed all the manifestations of the sun which paid homage to the Queen of Heaven and earth, more brilliant than the heavenly body itself at its zenith of light.

This phenomenon, which was not registered in any astronomical observatory, and could not, therefore, have been of natural origin, was witnessed by people of every category and class, by believers as well as unbelievers, journalists of the principal daily papers and even by people kilometres away, a fact which destroys any theory of collective hallucination.

(D. José Alves Correia da Silva, Bishop of Leiria, from a Pastoral Letter)

When Lucia called out, "Look at the sun!" the whole multitude echoed, "Look at the sun!" It was a day of incessant drizzle but a few moments before the miracle it left off raining. I can hardly find words to describe what followed. The sun began to move and at a certain moment appeared to be detached from the sky and about to hurtle on us like a wheel of flame. My wife - we had been married only a short time - fainted. I fell on my knees oblivious of everything and when I got up I don't know what I said. I think I began to cry out like the others.
(Senhor Alfredo de Silva Santos)

We looked easily at the sun which did not blind us. It seemed to flicker on and off, first one way and then another. It shot rays in different directions and painted everything in different colours - the trees, the people, the air and the ground. What was the most extraordinary was that the sun did not hurt our eyes at all. Everything was still and quiet; everyone was looking upwards. At a certain moment the sun seemed to stop and then began to move and to dance until it seemed that it was being detached from the sky and was falling on us. It was a terrible moment.
(Ti Marto, father of Francisco and Jacinta.)

The sun trembled, made sudden incredible movements outside all cosmic laws - the sun "danced" according to the typical expression of the people. They began to ask each other what they had seen. The great majority admitted to having seen the trembling and the dancing of the sun; others affirmed that they saw the face of the Blessed Virgin; others, again, saw that the sun whirled on itself like a giant catherine wheel and that it lowered itself to the earth as if to burn it in its rays. Some said they saw it change colours successively.
(Avelino de Almeida in the Seculo newspaper)

I saw the sun describe a swift circle, pause, describe another, pause again and describe a third. Then the clouds began to sweep over it again. Someone pulled my sleeve. It was an ancient crone, her face alight. "Do you see the roses falling?" she asked. She saw them, but for me, there in the mud, there were no roses, only a sense of disappointment. I had hoped for, half expected, a vision, compelling, all powerful, such as St Paul saw on the road to Damascus; something that would change one's life completely. Perhaps this was presumption. Perhaps just ignorance. What it was makes no difference, neither does what I felt or thought. Our Lady knew her people.
(Mabel Norton, a young Englishwoman then in service in Portugal. At the time she was not a Catholic, though she later converted and became a staunch Fatima champion.)

Suddenly the rain stopped and the sun broke through, casting its rays on the earth. It seemed to be falling on that vast crowd of people and it spun like a fire-wheel, taking on all the colours of the rainbow. We ourselves took on those colours, with our clothes and even the earth itself. One heard cries and saw many people in tears. Deeply impressed, I said to myself: "My God, how great is your power!"
(Dona Maria do Carmo da Cruz Menezes)

At one o'clock in the afternoon, midday by the sun, the rain stopped. The sky, pearly grey in colour, illuminated the vast arid landscape with a strange light. The sun had a transparent gauzy veil so that the eyes could easily be fixed upon it. The grey mother-of-pearl tone turned into a sheet of silver which broke up as the clouds were torn apart and the silver sun, enveloped in the same gauzy grey light, was seen to whirl and turn in the circle of broken clouds. A cry went up from every mouth and people fell on their knees on the muddy ground.

The light turned a beautiful blue as if it had come through the stained-glass windows of a cathedral and spread itself over the people who knelt with outstretched hands. The blue faded slowly and then the light seemed to pass through yellow glass. Yellow stains fell against white handkerchiefs, against the dark skirts of the women. They were repeated on the trees, on the stones and on the serra. People wept and prayed with uncovered

heads in the presence of a miracle they had awaited. The seconds seemed like hours, so vivid were they.
(From the O Dia newspaper 17.10.17.)

Francisco, 11 June 1908 - 4th April 1919

Francisco was to die just a month or so short of two years after the first Apparition of Our Lady at Cova da Iria.

Nothing spectacular happened on the outward surface of these two years, nothing worth noting, except, perhaps, an encounter with the devil that Lucia records in the Memoirs:

"One day we went to a place called Pedreira, and while the sheep were grazing, we jumped from rock to rock, making our voices echo down the deep ravines. Francisco withdrew, as was his wont, to a hollow among the rocks. A considerable time had elapsed, when we heard him shouting and crying out to us and to Our Lady. We ran in search of him, calling out his name.

'Where are you?'

'Here! Here!'

'At last we came upon him, trembling with fright, still on his knees.

'What's wrong? What happened to you?'

'It was one of those huge beasts that we saw in hell. He was right there, breathing out flames!'

"I saw nothing, neither did Jacinta, so I laughed and said to him: 'You never want to think about hell, so as not to be afraid; and now you're the first one to be frightened!'"

Francisco fell sick with the Spanish 'Flu which was then sweeping through Europe and taking more bodies to the grave than the First World War managed in its five horrific years. He was to spend six months on his death-bed, six months of continual prayer and constant sacrifices. On the 2nd April 1919 he made his first confession. On the following day he received the Body of Christ as Holy Viaticum. It was his First Communion. He died on 4th April at ten o'clock in the morning. His mother testified at the Parochial Inquiry: "He gave a smile and remained like that. Then he breathed no more." His father said, "He died smiling."

He was just a couple of days short of being the same age as Lucia was on the day of the first Apparition.

Francisco's remains were buried in the Fatima cemetery. In 1935 Jacinta's body was brought from the private burial grounds of Baron Alvaiázere in Ourem and interred in the same mausoleum that held Francisco's.

On 1st May 1951 Jacinta's remains were transferred to the Basilica and buried in the left transept as one faces the altar. Francisco's couldn't be found. Since many children died of the Spanish 'Flu, there were a number of bodies buried in the same grave. The box alongside which Jacinta had been buried, and which was thought to contain Francisco's bones, was examined by doctors who declared that they were the remains of a child of only a few months.

Francisco's father insisted that Francisco had been buried in that spot. Other bones were found, but for various reasons none of them could have been Francisco's. His father said that the body had been forced into the coffin because the measurements he had given the undertaker had been too small. In February 1952 the authorities dug the grave up again, this time going deeper. At length they came across a coffin tied with yellow braid which Ti Marto immediately recognised as his son's. The bone rosary beads he had been buried with were entwined between the finger bones and after examination doctors confirmed that the body was that of a male child between ten and thirteen years of age.

These remains were transferred to an urn and buried in the Basilica on the 13th March 1952, in the right transept as one faces the altar. The inscription reads:

Here Rest the Mortal Remains of Francisco Marto,
to whom Our Lady appeared

There is a tendency among devotees of Fatima to think of Jacinta as superior to Francisco, as if Francisco, although Jacinta's elder brother, was spiritually a poor cousin who happened to be present when the Lady appeared to the girls, who was borne along on the tide of the events ever since. "The Church is only beatifying Francisco," some people seem to think, "because of

Jacinta; she suffered longer and her body was incorrupt. By himself, Francisco would never be remembered." It is as if the siblings were a double act with their agents squabbling over billing.

By himself, Francisco would never have been remembered. No sweeter words could have been heard by the boy as he lay on his deathbed in the family cottage in Aljustrel, because the workings of grace had transformed his soul into a vessel such as centuries of contemplatives, of monks and nuns and a great army of lay folk, have striven and yearned and mortified themselves for - the bliss of being kidnapped by God.

The contemplative soul is not looking for a life of ease, for an on-going smorgasbord of spiritual delights. Nor is it looking for dark nights and great tempests of the soul, nor for a sweet disposition, friends, an aura of sanctity, martyrdom, canonisation. It is looking for its Creator to give itself to Him, a quest which would be futile and vainglorious except that the Creator wants it too, and runs the length of the universe to make Himself available. There He hovers under the guise of bread, offering love, a love so fearsome to the timid, flawed soul that it can only be caught in brief glimpses, yet so compelling that the soul is stunned to rapture.

Words like clever, entertaining, famous, haven't got an entry in the contemplative's lexicon. Fashion, excitement, novelty, are bizarre concepts. Love is the only word that identifies with The Word, the only word worth uttering and the only word worth listening to. To understand the motivation, the workings, the essence of contemplation, love is the word we must look up and ponder, but the only really satisfactory definition is in the loving.

Francisco, an illiterate peasant in ill-fitting trousers, who hadn't reached adolescence and had never heard the word 'contemplative', met these criteria, through grace, and in doing so achieved the unique position that his Creator had designed for him.

The more one studies Francisco the more clearly he comes into focus as a true contemplative. He couldn't hear what the Lady said and expressed no desire to do so because for some reason she didn't want him to. He didn't fret about the reason; her will was enough and he abandoned himself to it. The insults, the disbelief, the misunderstanding of the neighbours no doubt affected him as much as they did Lucia and Jacinta but Lucia records no memorable comment from Francisco on the subject because, we might assume, he was too preoccupied in burning his humiliation as fuel to console the offended Jesus.

One lesson of Francisco's life is his constant thinking of heaven, yearning for heaven, living, as it were, in heaven. If heaven is the goal, the boy seems to be saying, there is no point in wasting time dribbling the ball around centre field or cutting a smart figure before the spectators.

The action takes place on the field of prayer, the rule-book is found in the Mysteries of the Rosary. The Joyful Mysteries, home and village life, teach the tactics of humility. The Sorrowful Mysteries, the suffering, chosen and imposed, are the fight, but the Glorious are the object, the reason, the fulfilment of all. The goal justifies whatever takes place on the pitch; if your whole attention is focused there, everything else makes sense.

He never analyses. He senses love and in responding to this love he seems, in some extraordinary way, to disappear from view. His complete absence of worldly ambition, his own assumption that he is the least important of the seers, conforms with a mentality prescribed by St Benedict for the formation of contemplatives.

Francisco's lack of self-interest, together with his secret prayer life are of a piece with the prototypes of the Christian contemplative like Benedict Joseph Labre, Charles de Foucauld and Therésè Martin. The symptoms are the same. The thirst for solitude, the hours hidden camouflaged in prayer, the absorption in the Divine that go unremarked by those around because of the veil of paradox, the veil that enables the contemplative to disappear into prayer, into the very wood of the cross, to contemplate the sun at midnight and to stake all on a virgin with a child.

The symptoms are crystallised in the steps of humility as written down by Benedict for his monks: "When these steps have been mounted he acts now, not through fear of hell, but for the love of Christ, out of good habit and delight in virtue. All this Our Lord will work by the Holy Spirit in his servant." Here we have the proof of the true contemplative, the touchstone of canonisable sanctity. Miracles and wonders aren't often the province of the true contemplative. Should they be associated with him after his death this is but the joy God has of him, spilling over.

Jacinta, 11 March 1910 - 20 February 1920

Jacinta caught the Spanish 'Flu a month or so before Francisco. Indeed, the entire family was ill with the exception of Ti Marto, the father of the seers. Unlike Francisco, however, the course of Jacinta's illness was erratic. In the early stages she was sometimes able to get up and walk about, but mostly she was confined to bed. With the bronchial pneumonia a purulent abscess formed in the pleura, the membrane covering the lungs, which caused acute pain and emitted an unpleasant odour like putrefaction.

Three months after Francisco's death her condition was so bad that she was taken to St Augustine's hospital at Ourem. She was to stay there, deprived of her family apart from the occasional visit from her mother and Lucia, for two months. By the end of August 1918 it was clear that hospital treatment was having no effect and, anyway, the family could no long afford to pay the bills so she was brought back to Aljustrel.

The state of her small body, with tuberculosis now compounding the pleurisy, must have been terrible indeed. Dr. Formigão confirms that she was like a skeleton, the Koch Bacillus having eaten away at her flesh, leaving little more than skin and bone. The sufferings of this eight year old almost defy imagination. She told Lucia that she was offering her sufferings for the conversion of sinners. "I would give anything to be able to be able to go up to Cabeço and say a Rosary there in our favourite place! But I am not able for it any more. When you go to the Cova da Iria pray for me. Just think! I shall never go there again!" The tears, Lucia writes, streamed down her cheeks.

Our Lady visited Jacinta on a number of occasions during this protracted agony. The 'Public' Apparitions finished in October 1917, but the Immaculate Heart had promised never to abandon the children, a promise which she fulfilled abundantly in private. She revealed to Jacinta the course that the remainder of her short life would take. Jacinta repeated it to Lucia: "I am going to Lisbon to another hospital; I will not see you again, nor my parents either, and after suffering a great deal, I shall die alone. But she said I must not be afraid, since she herself is coming to take me to heaven."

This prospect of dying alone seemed to tear at her heart and cause even more intense suffering than the pain in her body. But Lucia tells that she would kiss the crucifix and exclaim, "O my Jesus! I love You, and I want to suffer very much for love of You. O Jesus! Now you can convert many sinners, because this is really a big sacrifice!"

Jacinta travelled to Lisbon with her mother and her brother Antonio at the beginning of January 1920. Initially they couldn't find anywhere to stay in Lisbon, which must have brought home the poignancy of Bethlehem to the poor family who had never been away from their Serra surroundings before. Eventually, however, they found shelter in an orphanage in the square named Estrella after the Basilica on the south side. This huge baroque church belongs to the Carmelites and features a statue of St Teresa of Àvila in a niche of the façade. The great reformer and mystic is holding a discipline in her hand but looks kindly and motherly and wise, almost as if she was expecting Jacinta.

This orphanage was called Our Lady of the Miracles. It was run by a nun whose name was Mother Maria de Purificação Godinho but who was also affectionately known as Madrinha - Godmother - to the children in her care. A contemporary photograph shows her to be a short, plump lady whom a visitor might expect to be the cook rather than the Superior. Or maybe she was both. She certainly made up for the inhospitality of the doors that had shut in the faces of the forlorn family from Aljustrel by extending a warm, maternal welcome.

Jacinta's mother stayed a week with her in the orphanage while arrangements were being made for Jacinta's admission into Estafânia Hospital in central Lisbon to be operated on for osteitis of the 7th and 8th ribs on her left side. Olimpia de Jesus Marto was reluctant to authorise an operation on her daughter whose tiny body had largely wasted away and was in continual pain. It was her husband's decision, she decided, and so set off on the journey back to Aljustrel leaving the suffering nine year old in the big city with nothing familiar but her precious "Hidden Jesus" in the Eucharist.

In all Jacinta was only in the orphanage for a couple of weeks or so, from the middle of January till the 2nd February 1920, yet the space she occupied still carries a distinctive stamp, a subtle aura of holiness, as if it were a kindergarten of heaven.

Today the building is a Poor Clare Convent, but Jacinta's bed and the rooms she used are preserved. Particularly of interest is the first floor grille choir window that gives onto the small Church of the Miracles next door. Here the suffering Jacinta would spend many hours seated in a chair looking down onto the tabernacle. And every day she had the joy of receiving the Blessed Sacrament, a privilege she had not had in Aljustrel and one which was not to be repeated in her last terrible two weeks in Estafânia Hospital.

Mother Godinho was astute enough to take notes of some of the seer's sayings when she was speaking with the other children. It is almost incredible that such mature wisdom was spoken spontaneously by a ten year old with almost no education, religious or secular. Consider observations such as:

"Doctors do not know how to cure people properly because they haven't the love of God."

"Many marriages are not of God and do not please Our Lord."

"Fashions will much offend Our Lord. People who serve God should not follow fashions:

Our Lord is always the same."

"Priests must be very, very pure."

"Priests should concern themselves only with things of the Church."

Should our own nine year olds be overheard remarking to their peers, "If the government would leave the Church in peace and give liberty to religion it would have God's blessing," or, "Wars are the punishment for sin" we might wonder if the manufacturers are putting quotes from Pascal or von Hugel in Christmas crackers these days. But Jacinta was listened to, and mature Religious took notes because she must have been surrounded with that air of authority that gives off truths as a welding rod gives off sparks from the mass it is fusing. She wasn't a nine year old being a "little Madam". She was a saint entering the final stage of her absorption into the wilderness of divine suffering, the marriage of spiritual annihilation, the longed-for face-to-face meeting with her Hidden Jesus.

We have it on the authority of Mother Godinho, and of Lucia, that Our Lady kept her promise not to abandon Jacinta by appearing to her on a number of occasions both at the orphanage and at Estafânia, and that she told Jacinta the day and the circumstances of her death.

On the 2nd of February, the Feast of the Presentation of Jesus in the Temple and the Purification of Our Lady, Jacinta moved from the orphanage to the hospital of Dona Estáfania. On the 10th the operation took place. It was performed by Dr Leonardo de Sousa Castro Freire, who was later to hold the Professorial Chair at Lisbon University's faculty of Medicine.

During the Process towards the Beatification of Jacinta, this Doctor gave testimony to Dom Alberto Cosme de Amaral, Bishop of Leiria-Fatima, in the presence of the Vice-Postulator, Father Luis Kondor. Here are some of the passages of the testament.

Dom Alberto: "In what circumstances did you know Jacinta?"

Dr. Leonardo: "When I met her I was paediatric Specialist and Professor Extraordinary at the Hospital of Dona Estefánia where I worked. She arrived at the hospital in a very serious condition and she had every appearance of suffering acutely. As a consequence of pneumonia, purulent pleurisy had developed. Also I found that two of her ribs had decayed..."

Dom Alberto: "It was you yourself who operated on Jacinta? Can you tell us something of the operation?"

Dr. Leonardo: "Yes. It was me who operated on Jacinta. The operation meant making an insertion large enough to drain off the pus and dry off the two ribs."

Dom Alberto: "When you operated on Jacinta did you know that she was one of the seers of Fatima?"

Dr. Leonardo: "No. I didn't know. It was much later that the nurse, Nadeje, said to me one day, 'This little girl is one of the visionaries of Fatima.'"

Dom Alberto: "Did anything about the way Jacinta comported herself impress you, during or after the operation?"

Dr. Leonardo: "She gave me the impression - always left me with the impression - of a child with much courage, and because she wasn't under a general anaesthetic, she wasn't immunised from the pain involved in the opening of the fistula etc. The only words I heard from her during the operation were these, 'Oh Jesus! O my God!'"

Dom Alberto: "In the light of all you have said are you able to affirm that Jacinta's patience was heroic?"

Dr. Leonardo: "Certainly, considering all she suffered and the way she suffered it. And also the fact that she was a child because, you know, an adult has more capacity for suffering than a child."

In spite of all the medical care the little one weakened and her state deteriorated until 20th February 1920.

At 6:00 in the afternoon she said that she felt very ill and asked for the sacraments. At 8:00 she made her confession to the Rev. Prior of the parish of the Angels, Monsignor Manuel Pereira dos Reis. She begged to be brought the Holy Viaticum because she was going to die. The priest, not discovering any signs of imminent death, decided to leave the Last Sacraments until the following day.

About 10:30 that night, Jacinta, a masterwork of Divine grace, one of the purest and most beautiful of souls who travelled through this world of sin, expired peacefully, alone, as Our Lady had foretold. She was still almost a year younger than Lucia had been at the time of the first Apparition.

Those whose reading takes them into the hearts of the saints will recognise a pattern in Jacinta's life: the total immolation, the *fiat* to the terrifying unknown when every feeling, inclination, emotion and reaction urges the contrary. The soul is alone, utterly vulnerable; it has nothing it can recognise except peace, the garment of faith, but even that seems far away, dormant in the core of being.

Jacinta, the 9 year old, has taken the torch from Therésè. As the world sinks deeper into the quagmire of sin, it would seem that the innocence of the young is becoming increasingly necessary as the burnt offering and atonement sacrifice of the new dispensation. It gives new meaning to the instruction of Jesus, "Unless you become as little children you shall not enter the kingdom of heaven." It still means to be trusting, certainly, and affectionate, and loyal and wide-eyed, but the King asks the children to pay towards the ransom of their elders who have laughed in His face and are sauntering off along the highway of greed.

To become a little child is also to be prepared to appease outraged love. It is all too easy to be fooled into cooing over pictures of a sweet Therésè holding a bunch of roses, or of Jacinta standing among her sheep smiling serenely at the Lady from Heaven. Through a mystery of grace which we cannot understand, both of them were nailed to the cross of Calvary, their bodies bloodied like the body of the Crucified Christ, and their spirits sharing in His desolation.

The life of every saint is a life of Jesus Christ.

Jacinta's sufferings, like Christ's, weren't the fear of pain or of death. Pain and death were as commonplace to her in bed N°60 Estafânia Hospital as bandages and bedpans. She had already died to this world but the horror that clamped her soul as her body lingered here, the horror beside which death was a door in out of the cold, was sin. It was the shadow of that ultimate evil that fell over Jacinta, and Therésè before her, and crushed their souls to the point where, if souls could die, they would have suffocated. Love rescued them. Love had gone on before and was waiting. Love held them very firmly and kissed them and transformed them into itself.

It is a gospel, always the same, always new.

Lucia, 22nd March 1906 - 13th February 2005

After the October Apparition Lucia was mostly in her family home in Aljustrel until she left for boarding school in Porto on June 16th 1921. During those years she saw Francisco die and, shortly after that, her father. The following year Jacinta died in Lisbon.

With her mother she went for a while to Valado as a guest of some ladies from Lisbon. From Valado they visited the fishing resort of Nazaré and the Cistercian Monastery at Alcobaça which dates from the 12th century and was modelled on St Bernard's own monastery, Clairvaux.

Back in Fatima the everlasting invasion of strangers wanting to question her continued. So when an invitation came, via the first chronicler of the Fatima phenomenon, Dr Formigão, from a lady in Lisbon called Dona Assunção Avelar to stay at her home, Lucia and her mother accepted. They remained there for some time, visiting, among other places, the orphanage in Estrella where Jacinta had stayed and the ward in Estafânia Hospital where she had died.

Lucia might have stayed on with Dona Assunção indefinitely, but the shell of her anonymity in Lisbon was beginning to crack. Agents of the anti-clerical government were aware that she was in the capital and, what with Dona Assunção being a fervent monarchist and consequently a threat in the eyes of the ruling Democrats, Lucia was taken to Dr. Formigão's home in Santarem.

There she attended Mass at the Church of the Miracle which houses a Sacred Host dating from the 13th century. She might have continued in Santarem, with a lady who lived next to the church who offered to keep and educate her, but the residents of Fatima were making a fuss. They resented the absence of their famous (albeit unwillingly) daughter, so it was decided that she should return home for a short while before starting school.

The Diocese of Leiria had been restored in 1918 - a move which was totally independent of the Apparitions -and the Bishop, José Alves Correia da Silva, arranged for Lucia to be brought to him. Indeed, Lucia confessed in the Cathedral before Mass without realising that her confessor was the Bishop. Later they spoke in private together and he suggested that she go to Porto to be educated in a boarding school there run by the Dorothean Sisters. No one at the school except the superiors would know who she was, and she would be protected from the never-ending cavalcade of curiosity seekers. From the Bishop's point of view, he could keep her under observation, as it were, while the claims of Fatima were being investigated.

Lucia's mother agreed that she could go on the condition that she could leave if she wasn't happy. Lucia would have preferred Santarem but consented

Sr. Lucia, visiting Fatima Parish Church, shortly after the beatification of Jacinta and Francisco, May 2000.

to the Porto proposition, as the Bishop's voice to her represented the Will of God.

And so on that June day in 1921 Lucia left Fatima for the College of the Dorothean Sisters in Vilar, near Porto. She used an assumed name, Maria dos Dores, Mary of the Sorrows.

When her schooling was finished she joined the Dorothean Congregation as a novice and was sent to their novitiate in Pontevedra in Spain.

On the 10th December 1925 when Lucia was in her room on the second storey of the Dorothean convent in Pontevedra, Our Lady appeared to her and, by her side, elevated on a luminous cloud, was a child. The Most Holy Virgin rested her hand on Lucia's shoulder and as she did so she showed her a heart encircled by thorns which she was holding in her other hand. At the same time the child said, "Have compassion on the Heart of your Most Holy Mother, covered with thorns, with which ungrateful men pierce it at every moment, and there is no one to make an act of reparation to remove them."

Then the Most Holy Virgin said, "Look, my daughter, at my Heart, surrounded with thorns with which ungrateful men pierce me at every moment by their blasphemies and ingratitude. You can at least try to console me and say that I promise to assist at the hour of death, with the graces necessary for salvation, all those who, for five consecutive months, shall confess, receive Holy Communion, recite five decades of the Rosary, and keep me company for 15 minutes while meditating on the 15 mysteries of the Rosary, with the intention of making reparation to me."

In another encounter, when Our Lord appeared to Lucia in the garden of the convent at Pontevedra on 15th February 1926, he said, "It is true, my daughter, that many souls begin the First Saturdays, but few finish them, and those who do complete them do so in order to receive the graces that are promised thereby. It would please me more if they did five with fervour and with the intention of making reparation to the Heart of your heavenly Mother, than if they did fifteen in a tepid and indifferent manner."

Shortly after this Lucia was moved to Tuy, on the Spanish side of the Minho River. She made her first profession of religious vows on 3rd October 1928. On 13th June the following year she received a second communication from Our Lady, promised in July 1917 when she said, "I shall come to ask for the consecration of Russia to my Immaculate Heart."

Here is Lucia's own account: "I had asked for and obtained permission from my superiors to make a Holy Hour from 11pm to midnight during the night of Thursday-Friday. Being alone, I knelt in the middle of the balustrade which is in the centre of the chapel to recite, prostrate, the prayers of the angel. Feeling tired, I got up and continued to recite them with arms outstretched. The only light was that of the sanctuary lamp.

"Suddenly the whole chapel lit up as by a supernatural light, and there appeared on the altar a cross of light which rose up as far as the ceiling. In this very clear light one could see on the upper part of the cross the figure of a man from the waist upwards, and on his chest was the figure of a dove, also luminous. Nailed to the cross was another man. A little below his waist, suspended in the air, one could see a chalice and a large host upon which there fell several drops of blood which flowed upon the cheeks of the crucified one, and from a wound in his chest. Flowing over the host, these drops fell into the chalice.

"Under the right arm of the cross was Our Lady (it was Our Lady of Fatima with her Immaculate Heart in her left hand without sword or roses, but with a crown of thorns and flames). Under the left arm of the cross, large letters of crystalline water flowed down over the altar and formed these words GRACE AND MERCY. I understood that the mystery of the Most Holy Trinity had been shown to me and I received enlightenment upon this mystery which is not permitted to me to reveal.

"Our Lady then said to me, 'The moment has come in which God asks the Holy Father, in union with all the Bishops of the world, to make the consecration of Russia to my Immaculate Heart, promising to save it by this means. There are so many souls whom the justice of God condemns for sins committed against me, that I have come to ask for reparation: sacrifice yourself for this intention and pray.' "

Later, through an intimate communication in August 1931, Our Lord complained: "They have not chosen to heed my request ... Like the King of France, they will regret it and then will do it, but it will be too late. Russia will already have spread her errors throughout the world, provoking wars and persecutions against the Church. The Holy Father will have much to suffer." Commentators interpret the reference to the King of France to refer to the failure of Louis XIV to consecrate France to The Sacred Heart, as revealed by St Margaret Mary Alacoque. The French Revolution was the outcome.

Lucia made her final vows as a Dorothean in Tuy on 3rd October 1934. Her mother travelled there for the occasion but it was the last time they were to meet. Her mother died in Aljustrel on 16th July 1942, the feast of Our Lady of Carmel, who had appeared to Lucy in the sky during the Miracle of the Sun.

On 25th January 1938, the night was illumined by an unknown light - which Our Lady had foretold during the July 1917 Apparition - which was seen all over Europe and recorded in all the observatories. Contemporary descriptions speak of this atmospheric phenomenon as a blood-red glow and a red rainbow. Emphasis was also put on the terrible impression that this aurora had made on individuals. In France it was particularly noticeable in the Alps and in Brittany where people concluded that a second world war was at hand.[3]

On 31st October 1942 Pope Pius XII consecrated the world to the Immaculate Heart of Mary in a Portuguese language radio broadcast. He didn't specifically mention Russia, which might have been politically imprudent at the time, but referred to "those peoples separated by error and discord". Lucia later commented, however, that the consecration was not in accord with what Our Lady had asked for in as much as it lacked the participation of the Bishops representing the entire body of the Faithful.

On 13th May 1946, the Papal Legate, Cardinal Masella, crowned Our Lady of Fatima Queen of the World on behalf of Pope Pius XII.

On the 25th May 1946 Lucia was posted to the College of the Sacred Heart of Jesus of Sardão in Vila Nova de Gaia, across the river from Porto.

Having obtained permission from Pius XII to embrace the contemplative life, she entered the Carmelite Convent in Coimbra on 25th March 1948. As a Carmelite she is known as Sister Maria Lucia of the Immaculate Heart.

At the close of the extended 1950 Holy Year, which took place in Fatima on October 13th 1951, Cardinal Tedeschini, the Papal Legate, revealed to an immense crowd that Pius XII had seen a repetition of the 1917 solar miracle in the Vatican Gardens on the eve of November 1st 1950, the day of the promulgation of the dogma of the Corporal Assumption of the Blessed Virgin Mary.

One attempt by Pope John XXIII in 1960 to make the consecration to the Immaculate Heart in the Sanctuary at Fatima failed to meet Our Lady's conditions because, although the Bishop of Leiria had written to all the bishops of the world, the Holy Father was not present himself, having sent a delegate.

In 1965 Pope Paul VI made an unexpected consecration at the last assembly of the Vatican II Council. Although the Bishops were present it did not fulfil the terms of Our Lady's request because their participation was not solicited.

On 13th May 1982 Pope John Paul II made a consecration in Fatima when offering his would-be assassin's bullet to the shrine, but as this, too, was without the participation of the Bishops, Sister Lucia said that it was invalid.

On the feast of the Annunciation, March 25th 1984, in Rome, kneeling before the same statue of Our Lady of Fatima which is venerated in the Chapel of the Apparitions, Pope John Paul II renewed the Consecration of the World to the Immaculate Heart of Mary, with substantially the same formula he used in Fatima on 13th May 1982. This 1984 consecration in Rome, made in union with bishops all over the world, corresponded exactly with the form of union that Our Lady had requested.

The then Bishop of Leiria-Fatima, Alberto Cosme do Amaral, who was in Rome for the Ceremony later said, "During the actual Consecration there were a few moments of pause during which it was not clear what the Holy Father said. Later I thanked the Pope for consecrating the world to the Immaculate Heart of Mary and the Pope added, 'and Russia!'" Bishop Amaral continued with a telling sentence, "A moral totality of the world's bishops joined the Pope in this collegial consecration, including Eastern Orthodox Bishops."

In 1992 the writer on Fatima, Carlos Evaristo, asked Sister Lucia in the Coimbra Carmel, "But did not Russia have to be specifically mentioned, and did not Our Lady say this?" The seer answered, "The Pope's intention was Russia, when he said, "those peoples..." in the text of the 1984 consecration. Those who knew of the request for the consecration of Russia, knew what he was referring to, as did God, who is all-knowledgeable and can read the minds of men. God knew that the Pope's intention was Russia and that he meant Russia in the consecration. What is important is the intention, like when a priest has the intention to consecrate a Host. Our Lady never requested that Russia be specifically mentioned by name. At the time I didn't even know what Russia was. We thought she was a very wicked woman. What matters is the Pope's intention, and the Bishops knew the intention the Pope had was to consecrate Russia."

Also, after the Consecration, Sister Lucia was visited by the Apostolic Nuncio and, in an interview with her published in the Fatima Family Messenger, October 1989, she reported that he asked her, "Is Russia now consecrated?"

"Yes, now it is."

"Now we wait for the miracle?"

"God will keep his word."

Also in 1989 Sister Lucia wrote a private letter, which she later gave permission to be printed in the international Catholic journal, 30 Days, (issue of March 1990) in which she explained that previous consecrations had not been effective because they had not been carried out in union with all the bishops. The letter continues, "It was later made by the present Pontiff, John Paul II, on 25th March 1984, after he wrote to all the Bishops of the world, asking that each of them make the consecration in his own diocese with the people of God who had been entrusted to him. The Pope asked that the statue of Our Lady of Fatima be brought to Rome and he did it publicly in union with all the bishops who, with His Holiness, were uniting themselves with the people of God, the Mystical Body of Christ; and it was made to the Immaculate Heart of Mary, Mother of Christ and of His Mystical Body, so that, with her and through her with Christ, the consecration could be carried and offered to the Father for the salvation of humanity. Thus the consecration was made by His Holiness Pope John Paul II on 25th March 1984." (In other private correspondence

Sister Lucia further revealed that the 1984 consecration had prevented a nuclear war that would otherwise have taken place in 1985.)

The sudden evaporation of Soviet Commu-nism towards the end of the 20th century is too well known to need repeating here.

In March 2000 Sister Lucia was 93 years old.

In May 2000 she travelled to Fatima to be present when Pope John Paul II beatified Francisco and Jacinta on 13th May. She stayed at St Joseph's Carmel there for several days and visited her childhood parish church of St Anthony in Fatima on Tuesday 16th May.

Sr Lucia died at the age of 97 on Sunday 13th February 2005. In her last hours she was surrounded by her sisters in religion and the Bishop of Coimbra. Pope John Paul II said of her: "Sister Lucia leaves us an example of great fidelity to the Lord and of joyful adherence to his divine will."

Footnotes

(1) From the inception of the Portuguese nation the kings and people considered the Archangel Michael as "The guardian spirit who watches over, protects and defends the country". This is why King João II ordered the Archangel's image to be painted above the altar in the church of São Francisco in Évora and the artist instructed to have the Archangel bearing the shield of Portugal on his arm. King Manuel I asked Pope Leo X if a feast of the Guardian Angel of the Kingdom might be instituted. When the feast was granted it was celebrated by processions throughout the whole country. From the 16th to the 18th century devotion to the Angel of Portugal was magnificent, deep and lively, always accompanied by liturgical celebrations and great rejoicing. Inexplicably the feast began to lose its popularity and disappear in the second half of the 19th century, except in Braga where it is still celebrated on 9th July.

(2) Conversations with Our Lady always seem to be so courteous on both sides. It is said that when Our Lady appeared to Juan Diego in Guadaloupe, Mexico, she addressed him in his language, Nahuatl, and introduced herself by saying: "I have the great honour of being the Mother of God, and I beg the honour to be your mother too". In his reply, Juan Diego used an idiomatic form of address and called her his "beautiful daughter". - Source: Paul McLeod, Geelong, Australia.

(3) An article in the British journal The New Scientist for 14.4.83 called Dragon-slaying by John H. Parkinson reads: "Aurorae have not just been mistaken for dragons. A particularly brilliant display in January 1938, was interpreted by some people as the fulfilment of a prophecy of Our Lady of Fatima, that 'the chastisement of the world was at hand'. Indeed, three months later, Hitler invaded Austria." Here in Britain some bright spark thought Windsor Castle was on fire and called the fire brigade.

Sources

The chief source for this pamphlet has been *Memórias da Irmã Lúcia*, edited by Fr Luis Kondor SVD and translated into English by the Dominican nuns of the Perpetual Rosary, of the Pius XII Monastery in Fatima. Any extra material pertaining to the apparitions has been taken from *Documentação Crítica de Fatima* Vols I & II as published by the Santuário de Fatima. These extracts have been acknowledged in the text. Cardinal Sodano's speech regarding the "third" secret of Fatima delivered after the Mass following the Beatification of Francisco and Jacinta Marto is quoted on pages 37-39. My thanks to SOUL Magazine for permission to quote from articles which have appeared under my own name. Personal opinions are submitted to the judgement of the Church.

AN YOU TRUST GOD?

DR. TIM GRAY

Dr. Gray addresses the pervasive misconceptions that God is quick to anger, that the God of the Old and New Testaments are different, and that God doesn't have a merciful heart for us.

MEN AND WOMEN ARE FROM EDEN

DR. MARY HEALY

With incredible clarity, Dr. Healy explains how the *Theology of the Body* is astonishingly good news for a culture littered with broken marriages, immorality, heartache, and loneliness.

To learn more, visit us at
augustineinstitute.org/audio
or call (866) 767-3155